Rookie National Parks™

Acadia National Park

by Audra Wallace

Content Consultant
National Park Service

Reading Consultant
Jeanne M. Clidas, Ph.D.
Reading Specialist

Children's Press®
An Imprint of Scholastic Inc.

Library of Congress Cataloging-in-Publication Data
Names: Wallace, Audra, author.
Title: Acadia National Park/by Audra Wallace.
Description: New York, NY: Children's Press, an imprint of Scholastic Inc., 2018.
Series: Rookie national parks | Includes index.
Identifiers: LCCN 2017023147 | ISBN 9780531231937 (library binding) | ISBN 9780531230923 (pbk.)
Subjects: LCSH: Acadia National Park (Me.)—Juvenile literature.
Classification: LCC F27.M9 W35 2018 | DDC 974.1/45—dc23
LC record available at https://lccn.loc.gov/2017023147

Produced by Spooky Cheetah Press
Design: Judith Christ-Lafond/Ed LoPresti Graphic Design

Published in 2018 by Children's Press, an imprint of Scholastic Inc.

Printed in Heshan, China 62

1 2 3 4 5 6 7 8 9 10 R 27 26 25 24 23 22 21 20 19 18

Photographs ©:cover: Kim Seng/CaptainKimo.com; back cover: Fotosearch RM/age fotostock; cartoon fox throughout: Bill Mayer; 1-2: PCRex/Shutterstock; 3: BlueGreen Pictures/Superstock, Inc.; 4-5: Fotosearch RM/age fotostock; 6 background, 7: John Greim/Getty Images; 6 inset: Neil Rabinowitz/Getty Images; 8: Gabe Souza/Portland Press Herald/Getty Images; 10 background, 11: Richard Freeda/Getty Images; 10 inset: Greg A. Hartford/Acadia Magic; 12 background, 13: SuperStock/age fotostock; 12 inset: Walter Bibikow/age fotostock; 14: Patryce Bak/Getty Images; 15: Joseph Van Os/Getty Images; 16: Danita Delimont/Alamy Images; 17: GDacey/iStockphoto; 18-19 background: DougLemke/iStockphoto; 18 inset: Underwood & Underwood/Transcendental Graphics/Getty Images; 19 inset: Megapress/Alamy Images; 20: Minden Pictures/Superstock, Inc.; 21: Robin Chittenden/NPL/Minden Pictures; 22-23 background: Francois Gohier/ardea.com/age fotostock; 22 boat: Flip Nicklin/Minden Pictures/Superstock, Inc.; 23 inset: Nancy Elwood-Naturesportal/Getty Images; 24 background, 25: Richard Freeda/Getty Images; 24 inset: Jerry Monkman/Aurora Photos; 26 top left: Michel Gunther/Biosphoto/Minden Pictures; 26 top center: Isselee/Dreamstime; 26 top right: MYN/Les Meade/NPL/Minden Pictures; 26 bottom left: Jim Cumming/Shutterstock; 26 bottom center: Rob & Ann Simpson/Getty Images; 26 bottom right: Dorling Kindersley/Getty Images; 27 top left: Mark Raycroft/age fotostock; 27 top center: Alexander Raths/Shutterstock; 27 top right: FLPA/Paul Hobson/Superstock, Inc.; 27 bottom left: FRANKHILDEBRAND/iStockphoto; 27 bottom center: tonguy324/iStockphoto; 27 bottom right: cris180/iStockphoto; 30 top left: Matthew Ward/Getty Images; 30 top right: DEA/G. NEGRI/Getty Images; 30 bottom left: LisaChristianson/iStockphoto; 30 bottom right: Wally Eberhart/Getty Images; 31 top: Pat & Chuck Blackley/Alamy Images; 31 center top: elmvilla/iStockphoto; 31 bottom: f11photo/Shutterstock; 31 center bottom: DougLemke/iStockphoto; 32: Danita Delimont Stock/AWL Images.

Maps by Jim McMahon.

Table of Contents

I am Ranger Red Fox, your tour guide. Are you ready for an amazing adventure in Acadia?

Welcome to Acadia National Park!

Acadia (uh-**kay**-dee-uh) is in Maine and was made a **national park** in 1916. People visit national parks to explore nature.

The Rockefellers, one of America's richest families, helped create Acadia. For more than 100 years, the family has continued to give money and land to the park.

United States

Maine →

Acadia
National Park

N W E S

There are many fun things to do in Acadia. You can climb high cliffs and visit a lighthouse. You can even ride a horse-drawn carriage through the forest. Be sure to bring your flip-flops, because Acadia has beaches, too!

The Bass Harbor Head Lighthouse was built in 1858.

Acadia was the first national park on the east coast of the United States.

During fall and winter, Cadillac Mountain is the first place you can see the sunrise in the U.S.

Every day in August, between 400 and 600 people climb Cadillac Mountain.

Chapter 1

An Icy Past

For millions of years, much of Earth was freezing cold. During this Ice Age, huge sheets of ice moved over parts of the planet. These **glaciers** smoothed out Acadia's rocky mountaintops. One of those mountains is Cadillac Mountain.

Cadillac Mountain is the tallest mountain in the park. It is 1,530 feet (466 meters) tall, which makes it taller than most skyscrapers.

A glacier also cut through Mount Desert Island. It left behind a **fjard** called Somes Sound.

Somes Sound is one of just two fjards on the east coast of the U.S.

The glaciers carried big rocks with them. Bubble Rock is a giant stone that ended up on the edge of a cliff. It has been there for thousands of years.

Bubble Rock weighs 100 tons, which is 14 times as heavy as an elephant.

The spot where these people are standing is often covered in water!

Chapter 2

Seaside Sights

Ice is not the only thing that shaped Acadia. Powerful waves from the Atlantic Ocean did, too. The waves made holes, called sea caves, in the cliffs along the shore.

The most famous sea cave is Thunder Hole. It sounds like thunder when a big wave smashes into it and the air trapped inside is forced out.

In winter, the ocean spray freezes on Otter Cliff. That doesn't stop climbers, though!

Crashing waves helped form Otter Cliff.

Acadia is home to many beaches. Most are covered by gravel and small stones. Some are covered with cobblestones, and a few have sand.

The park is also home to Otter Cliff. At 110 feet (34 meters) tall, it is one of the highest cliffs on the Atlantic coast. Climbing Otter Cliff is not easy. Crashing waves can make the cliff very slippery.

Some cobblestones are as big as basketballs!

Chapter 3

That's Wild!

Not all of Acadia's sights are by the sea. Visitors hike, bike, and ride horses through the forests. They travel on stone trails called carriage roads.

Stone bridges are also found in the park. Some go over roads. Others cross over streams.

There are 45 miles (72 km) of carriage roads in Acadia.

There are 16 stone carriage road bridges in Acadia.

John D. Rockefeller Jr. built the park's first carriage roads near his home. He wanted to ride his horse and carriage on them.

Native Americans once used paper birch to make baskets and canoes. Paper birch canoes are light but strong.

Acadia's forests are filled with different kinds of trees. One of the most common is paper birch. Other types of trees include spruce, fir, sugar maple, red oak, and poplar.

In spring, wildflowers bloom in the meadows. Plants like water lilies and cattails grow in **marshes** and ponds.

Water lilies grow in Acadia's ponds.

In summer, you can pick blueberries along the park's trails.

The moose is Maine's state animal.

Chapter 4

Acadia's Animals

You may see white-tailed deer nibbling on the grass in Acadia. Black bears and moose live in the park, too. But they are rarely seen.

The peregrine falcon is one of the fastest animals on Earth.

More than 300 types of birds live in Acadia. One of them is the peregrine falcon. It builds its nest high in the cliffs.

Many animals live in the ocean near Acadia. People go on boat trips to get a closer look.

Seals and dolphins play in the waves. Humpback whales leap into the air.

Visitors can take whale-watching trips in Maine.

Some visitors are lucky enough to see Atlantic puffins. These birds hang out on small islands in the sea.

An Atlantic puffin can hold more than 10 fish in its mouth at one time!

Acadia is busiest in July, August, and September.

More than two million people visit Acadia each year. This beautiful park is often called the crown jewel of Maine. It is the only place on the east coast of the United States where the mountains are so close to the sea.

Imagine you could visit Acadia. What would you do there?

These are just some of the incredible animals that make their home in or near Acadia.

snapping turtle

Atlantic puffin

bullfrog

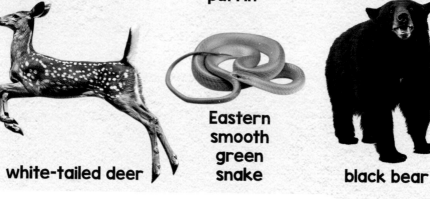

white-tailed deer

Eastern smooth green snake

black bear

Wildlife by the Numbers

The park is home to about...

364 types of birds   **55** types of mammals

Acadia is a great place for bird-watching!

moose

Atlantic salmon

river otter

peregrine falcon

humpback whale

spotted salamander

26 types of reptiles and amphibians

33 types of fish

Where Is Ranger Red Fox?

Oh no! Ranger Red Fox has lost his way in the park. But you can help. Use the map and the clues below to find him.

1. Ranger Red Fox woke up early to see the sunrise from Cadillac Mountain.

2. Then he hiked southeast to the beach. The sand felt very crunchy beneath his paws.

3. Next, he headed south to climb a tall cliff. He could not believe he made it to the top!

4. Finally, he made his way to a waterway formed by a glacier.

Help! Can you find me?

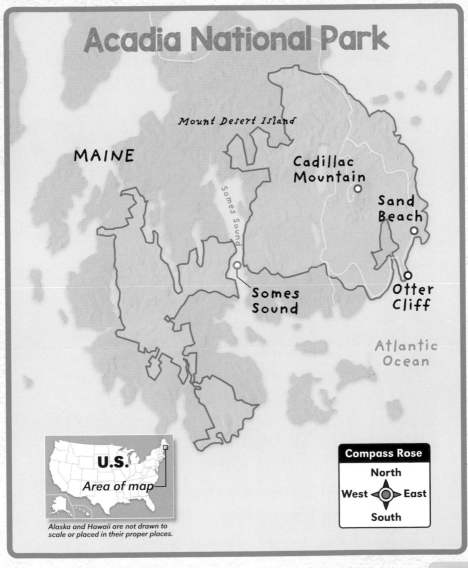

Acadia National Park

Mount Desert Island

MAINE

Cadillac Mountain

Sand Beach

Somes Sound

Somes Sound

Otter Cliff

Atlantic Ocean

U.S.
Area of map

Alaska and Hawaii are not drawn to scale or placed in their proper places.

Compass Rose

North

West — East

South

Leaf Tracker

Can you guess which leaf belongs to which tree in Acadia? Read the clues to help you.

A.

1. Sugar maple
Clue: This tree has leaves with five "fingers" and pointy edges.

B.

2. White pine
Clue: This tree has leaves that are long and thin, like needles.

3. Red oak
Clue: The leaves of this tree have seven to nine "fingers" with pointed edges.

C.

4. Paper birch
Clue: The leaves of this tree are rounded on the bottom. Their tips are pointy like a triangle.

D.

30

Glossary

fjard (**fy**-ard): short ocean inlet within a valley surrounded by mountains

glaciers (**glay**-shurz): huge blocks of slow-moving ice

marshes (**marsh**-ez): areas of wet, muddy land

national park (**nash**-uh-nuhl pahrk): area where the land and its animals are protected by the U.S. government

Index

Facts for Now

Visit this Scholastic Web site for more information
on Acadia National Park:
www.factsfornow.scholastic.com
Enter the keyword Acadia

About the Author

Audra Wallace is an editor at Scholastic. She lives with her family in New York. She enjoys going on adventures with them, but she is very afraid of heights!